GARETH BALE

THE ULTIMATE FAN BOOK

Iain Spragg

CARLTON
BOOKS

CONTENTS

Gareth Bale has come a long way since the youngster first kicked a ball growing up in his hometown of Cardiff, dreaming of a professional football career. Everyone who saw him play back then knew he had outrageous natural talent but even his closest family and friends could not have guessed what a global superstar he would become.

Today Bale is one of the game's most feared and famous players and watching the flying Welshman in full flow is one of football's finest sights. When Bale is on top form, opposition defences are powerless to stop him.

His incredible journey from Cardiff to Real Madrid, signing for the La Liga giants in a world record £85.3million deal in the summer of 2013, took him first to Southampton and then to the Premier League with Tottenham, but it is since he arrived in Spain that Bale has matured into a truly world-class performer.

Blessed with incredible pace, power and a lethal left foot, the Welshman has already helped Los Blancos win seven major trophies, including three Champions Leagues and La Liga in 2016–17. With a new contract that will keep him at the club until 2022, more silverware is only a matter of time.

The Bernabeu faithful have fallen in love with the flying winger since his transfer and he is already a club legend as he aims to join an exclusive group of players to score more than 100 goals for Real.

At international level Bale is a multiple record-breaker for Wales and it was his seven goals in qualification that booked his country's place at Euro 2016, the first time the country had reached the finals of a tournament in 58 years. Bale was even better in France, top scoring with three goals in the group stages as Wales tore up the formbook and made it all the way to the semi-finals.

Gareth Bale was Wales's star player at the finals of Euro 2016 in France.

Since signing for Real Madrid in 2013 Bale has lifted the Champions League trophy three times, including in 2016.

THE EARLY YEARS

A brilliant young sportsman, Bale's natural talent was first spotted before he'd even celebrated his tenth birthday.

Gareth Frank Bale was born in Cardiff in July 1989 and it probably came as little surprise to his parent Frank and Debbie that their young son was a keen footballer. Bale's uncle Chris Pike was a professional footballer and it wasn't long before his nephew started to follow in his footsteps.

His big break came while he was in action for his local team Cardiff Civil Service. "I was about eight or nine," he said. "I was playing in a five-a-side tournament in Newport and there was a Southampton scout there. He came up to my dad and spoke to me a bit later on and invited me for a trial."

Bale was already on his way to stardom, but his all round ability saw him shine at a number of different sports at secondary school, including rugby and hockey, but it was athletics which really excited him. "I competed in everything, long distance, middle distance and sprinting," he said.

Bale grew up in Cardiff with his parents Frank and Debbie and sister Vicky.

"I won pretty much everything. I was better at long distance, but preferred doing the shorter distances. Sprinting was my favourite. I once ran the 100 metres in 11.4 seconds."

Bale attended Whitchurch High School at the same time as future Wales rugby captain Sam Warburton, but football remained his first love and he was so good at the game that the school PE teacher banned him from using his left foot in games to give the other children a chance.

By the age of 14 he was travelling every week from Cardiff to train with the Southampton junior teams. He left school in the summer of 2005 after helping the school's Under-18s win the Cardiff & Vale Senior Cup and went to live in England.

The only obstacle in his path to becoming a star was an ongoing back injury but once that was fixed, there was no stopping Bale. "I was quite small, then I had a big growth spurt that led to a problem with my back, which stopped me playing for a while," he said. "My bones were growing too quickly for my weight."

Bale won an FA Youth Cup runners-up medal with the Saints in 2005.

Wales rugby star Sam Warburton was in the same year as Bale at Whitchurch High School in Cardiff.

THE YOUNG SAINT

Bale signed his professional contract with Southampton and although he was still a teenager, he quickly broke in the first team at St Mary's.

When Bale left Wales for Southampton, he made an immediate impact at the club, helping the Saints win the 2005–06 Premier League Academy title, and it was not long before manager George Burley decided he was ready for the big time.

He was handed his debut in April 2006 in a Championship fixture against Millwall aged just 16 years and 275 days, becoming the second youngest player to pull on the shirt in the club's history. Bale's professional career was up and running.

He played twice in 2005–06 but it was the following season he really started to make the headlines as a regular starter for the Saints, featuring in 38 of the club's 46 Championship games as Southampton narrowly missed out on promotion to the Premier League.

Bale scored five times that year, his first senior goal coming in August against Derby County at Pride Park while he showcased his deadly ability with free-kicks three days later when he was on target against Coventry at St Mary's.

Everyone was now talking about the teenager and in December he won the BBC Wales Young Sports Personality of the Year award. In March 2007, he was voted the Football League Young Player of the Year and Bale was the name on everyone's lips.

Gareth Bale made his senior debut for Southampton in 2006 at the age of only 16.

The youngster scored five goals for Southampton in 2006–07, helping the team into the play-offs.

"I am absolutely thrilled," he said after picking up the second award. "I know I still have a lot to learn, so to get this is very special. Every time I think life can't get any better it does."

With Bale in dazzling form, the Saints made it through to the end-of-season play-offs, but he was injured in the second-half of the first leg against Derby and didn't play again that season. It was to be his final appearance for Southampton.

The Welsh teenager made 38 league appearances for the Saints in the 2006–07 season.

Bale was on his way to North London in 2007 when he signed for Spurs in a £7 million deal.

LEGEND AT THE LANE

Bale's stunning performances for Southampton in the Championship made him a transfer target for a host of Premier League clubs and it was Tottenham who won the race for the teenager's signature.

Talent is always in demand and when the biggest clubs in England were looking for new players in the summer of 2007, Bale's name was top of everyone's list. The young Welshman was hot property and although he was linked with moves to both Manchester United and Arsenal, he decided White Hart Lane was the place to be.

"I'm excited to be coming to a massive club like Spurs," the 17-year-old said. "It's pushing forward and I want to be part of its future. I really want to play in the Premiership. That's very important to me and this is a fantastic opportunity. I've thought long and hard about it and feel the time is right to move on."

The deal to sign Bale cost Tottenham £7million and although he took time to adapt to life in London and top-flight football, the fee turned out to be an amazing bargain.

At first playing in midfield, he made his debut against Manchester United at Old Trafford in August 2007 and, six days later, he scored his first goal for the club against Fulham. An ankle injury in December however brought his first season to a sudden and sad end.

He made 30 appearances in all competitions in 2008–09, 16 in the Premier League, mostly as a left-back, but it was the next year that Bale really made his big breakthrough, scoring the winning goals in London derbies against Arsenal and Chelsea in the space of three days in April. Those exploits earned him the Premier League Player of the Month award.

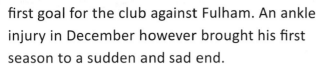

Bale's breakthrough season at White Hart Lane was in 2008–09 with the teenager making 30 appearances for the club.

Bale made a quick impact on the Premier League, scoring in only his second top-flight game.

Bale lit up Tottenham's UEFA Champions League adventure in 2010–11 with a brilliant hat-trick against Inter Milan.

His goals helped Tottenham qualify for the Champions League for the first time and it was his performances in Europe in 2010–11 which confirmed the Welshman genuinely was a world-class player.

Spurs were drawn against Inter Milan, Werder Bremen and FC Twente in the group stages of the competition and Bale was in red hot form against the Italian giants home and away, scoring the first hat-trick of his professional career in the first game in the San Siro. He was almost as deadly in the return at White Hart Lane, setting up two of his team's three goals as Tottenham ran out 3-1 winners.

"He plays left-back, wide left, he scores goals and runs all day," said manager Harry Redknapp after the first game. "Even in the first-half he gave the right-back, who is one of the best in the world, a torrid time. A year ago he was nowhere near that player we see now. He is developing every game and improving. Tottenham is where he belongs and where he will progress. There is no way the club will contemplate selling him."

With Bale in unstoppable form, Spurs – in their first appearance in Europe's top competition for 48 years – made it through to the quarter-finals. Although they were beaten by Real Madrid in the last eight, the youngster's brilliance had proved he could perform on the biggest stage in club football.

It was no surprise that the Welshman now started to collect individual awards. In April 2011 he was named the Professional Footballers' Association Player of the Year, the fourth Welshman to receive the honour, while in January 2012, he was included in the UEFA Team of the Year after his incredible performances in the Champions League.

The 2011–12 season was his best yet for Tottenham. He bagged 12 goals in all competitions, the second year in a row he had reached double figures, and with every big club in Europe watching him, Spurs handed him a new four-year contract to keep him at White Hart Lane.

Playing in the UEFA Champions League with Tottenham raised Bale's profile all across Europe.

Bale changed his shirt number at the start of the 2012–13 campaign from 3 to 11, because he wasn't "a left-back anymore" and with the freedom to get forward and attack, the star spent the whole season terrifying helpless Premier League defences.

He kicked-off his sensational scoring spree in September as Spurs beat Manchester United, the club's first win at Old Trafford for more than 20 years, and the goals just kept coming.

The first league hat-trick of his career was registered in December as Tottenham destroyed Aston Villa 4-0 at Villa Park, while he began an amazing run of form in January with another goal, against Norwich, the start of seven goals in five consecutive Premier League appearances that ended with another strike in a 2–1 victory over Arsenal at White Hart Lane in the north London derby. He wasn't finished yet and four more goals in Spurs' last six league games took his tally for the season to a career-best 21.

It was inevitable that Bale would pick up more awards after such an incredible year and in April 2013 he was named both the PFA Young Player of the Year and Player of the Year. A week later, there was more silverware as he was voted the Football Writers' Association Player of the Year, becoming only the second man after Cristiano Ronaldo in 2007 to lift all three awards in the same season.

"It means a lot to win this award when you consider the number of players that have been outstanding for their clubs in the Premier League this season," he said after picking up his third trophy.

"I have been very fortunate to be playing in such a fantastic team and I owe a lot to my team-mates and, obviously, the manager who has shown such faith in me. This award has been won in the past by some of the greatest names in football and I consider it a privilege that the FWA has selected me to be named alongside them."

Bale's ability to rip up even the meanest defence had made him the envy of every club in Europe and unfortunately for Spurs fans, a few months after his award treble and six brilliant seasons at the Lane their hero would be swapping the white of Tottenham for the white of Real Madrid.

Bale scored 26 goals in all competitions for Spurs in the 2012–13 season.

The Welshman was the standout player in England during the 2012–13 season.

Bale's final appearance for Tottenham came against Sunderland at White Hart Lane in May 2013.

PRIDE OF WALES

First capped as a teenager in 2006, Bale is on target to become his country's all-time record goal scorer.

It was only six weeks after Bale had made his senior debut for Southampton that Wales manager John Toshack called the youngster into his squad for a friendly against Trinidad & Tobago. Named a substitute, he sat on the bench for the first 55 minutes of the match but, when he came on in the second half, Bale became Wales' then youngest-ever international at the age of only 16 years and 315 days.

"It was exciting just warming up on the side and I was just wishing I could get on," Bale said. "I wasn't expecting all this, this year. I'm proud and so are my parents obviously. I just want to build on it from here. I enjoyed every minute."

Bale's international career has gone from strength to strength since that game more than 10 years ago. He netted his first goal for Wales in October 2006, a free-kick against Slovakia to become the country's youngest ever scorer. And, today, he is one of the most feared players in international football.

He has won the Wales Footballer of the Year Award a record six times, the first time in 2010, while in 2011 he was voted the BBC Wales Sports Personality of the Year.

Bale won his 50th cap in June 2015, in a Euro 2016 qualifier against Belgium, who were ranked number two in the world, and in his hometown of Cardiff he celebrated the occasion with a stunning solo goal to win the match. In total he scored seven times in qualifying, his strikes sending Wales to the finals of the European Championships for the first time in their history.

His brilliant form in front of goal continued as Wales began their 2018 World Cup qualifying campaign with four goals in his first four appearances. His goal in the 1–1 draw with Serbia in Cardiff in November 2016 took his international tally to 26 in 65 games, leaving him just two behind Ian Rush's record of 28 goals for Wales.

Gareth Bale was just 16 years old when he made his full international debut against Trinidad & Tobago.

The winger celebrated his 50th cap for his country in 2015 with a stunning winner against Belgium.

Bale, with 26 so far, seems destined to become Wales' all-time record goal-scorer, beating Ian Rush's total of 28.

GREAT SPURS GOALS

Here are six of Gareth Bale's best goals during his six seasons with Tottenham.

Bale ripped the Inter Milan defence to shreds in the San Siro in 2010.

STOKE CITY 1 v TOTTENHAM 2
Premier League, 21 August 2010

The Welshman scored twice to earn Spurs three points at the Britannia and his second was an unbelievable effort. Fellow midfielder Aaron Lennon supplied the cross and, standing just outside the six-yard box, Bale unleashed a brilliant, first-time volley that rocketed off his left boot and smashed into the top corner.

INTER MILAN 4 v TOTTENHAM 3
Champions League, 20 October 2010

Bale scored the first hat-trick of his career in the San Siro and the pick of his incredible treble in Italy was his first goal. Collecting the ball deep in his own half, he turned on the pace down the left wing, leaving three Inter players trailing behind him, and then drilled an unstoppable low, left-footed drive into the bottom corner.

NORWICH 0 v TOTTENHAM 2
Premier League, 27 December 2011

Bale's incredible speed created this goal at Carrow Road, but it was his superb technique that finished it off. Spurs broke from deep and the Welshman's scorching pace took him through the heart of the Norwich defence before he found the back of the net with a cool chip over the helpless keeper.

The Welshman is deadly from any range with his left foot from free-kick situations.

TOTTENHAM 2 v LYON 1
Europa League, 14 February 2013

The match was all-square at 1-1 at White Hart Lane and, in the 90th minute, Spurs were awarded a free-kick just outside the penalty area. Bale stepped forward and delivered a viciously bending shot which sailed over the wall and sent the Lyon goalkeeper completely the wrong way.

MANCHESTER CITY 3 v TOTTENHAM 2
Premier League, 22 January 2012

A goal which left the Etihad stunned in silence, Bale's 65th minute strike against City was amazing. He was outside the box when he received the ball and before the defence had time to react he produced a lethal, curling first-time shot which left England goalkeeper Joe Hart clutching thin air.

WEST HAM 2 v TOTTENHAM 3
Premier League, 25 February 2013

Spurs were pouring forward in search of a winner at Upton Park and the brilliant Bale dramatically supplied it in the 89th minute. His dazzling 40-yard shot gave goalkeeper Jussi Jaaskelainen no chance as it sailed past him and into the top of the net.

In all, Gareth Bale scored 55 goals in his six years in North London.

SPURS MILESTONES

MAY 2007
After only 45 first-team appearances for Southampton, signed for Tottenham in a four-year, £7million deal.

No amount of rain could dampen Bale's joy after he scored his first European goal against FC Twente.

AUGUST 2007
Made his debut for Tottenham in a Premier League clash with Manchester United. Five days later he scored his first goal in a 3–3 draw with Fulham at Craven Cottage.

SEPTEMBER 2007
His first European appearance is in Spurs' 6–1 defeat of Cyprus's Anorthosis Famagusta in the first round of the UEFA Cup.

MAY 2010
Signed a new four-year deal with the club.

SEPTEMBER 2010
Scored his first European goal in the 4–1 UEFA Champions League group stage defeat of FC Twente at White Hart Lane.

OCTOBER 2010
Registered his first hat-trick with a stunning second-half UEFA Champions League treble against Inter Milan in Italy.

DECEMBER 2010
On target against Newcastle in the league, he is into double figures for goals in a season for the first time.

DECEMBER 2010

APRIL 2011
Named the Professional Footballers' Association Player of the Year for the first time.

MARCH 2013
Scored his 50th Spurs goal in a Europa League clash against Inter Milan at the Lane.

APRIL 2013
Won his second PFA Player of the Year award, finishing ahead of Luis Suarez and Robin van Persie and is also named Football Writers Association Footballer of the Year and PFA Young Player of the Year.

MAY 2013
Made his 203rd and final appearance for the club, scoring the only goal in a win over Sunderland in the Premier League at White Hart Lane. It took his goal tally for the season to 26, making him Tottenham's top scorer.

AT HOME WITH BALE

When he's not lighting up the Bernabeu, Gareth Bale is a private person who loves to spend his free time with family and friends.

Bale might be one of the most famous footballers on the planet but when he's not in action for Real Madrid, he loves the simple life and can usually be found at home with his fiancée and two young daughters.

He met Emma Rhys-Jones when they were at Whitchurch High School in Cardiff in the early 2000s and the couple have been close ever since. They announced their engagement on 17 July 2016, the day after Bale's 27th birthday, and are planning to get married in the summer of 2017.

The couple have two daughters: Alba Violet was born in Cardiff in October 2012; and her sister, Nava Valentina, was born in March 2016. They live in the exclusive La Fincha district of Madrid but frequently fly back to Wales to see family and friends.

Daughter Alba celebrates with Dad after Wales' Euro 2016 win over Northern Ireland.

A keen golfer, Bale has built three holes of his own at his home in South Wales.

Gareth and Emma have been together since the pair meet at secondary school in Cardiff.

The star likes to keep his home life as private as possible, but Alba did make a surprise appearance during Euro 2016 in France when she ran onto the pitch wearing a Wales kit to celebrate with her dad after the team's victory over Northern Ireland in Paris.

His young family keeps Bale busy when he's not training or playing, but if he does have time he likes to indulge in his other passion away from football, which is golf.

There are plenty of courses in Madrid for the Welshman to play but, in 2015, he built himself a three-hole course in the back garden of his home in south Wales so he could hit a few balls whenever he liked.

"I love playing golf," he said. "I love the sport, I love the fact that you can just get away from everything, be with your friends, and no one can come over to you on a golf course. It's nice to get out and switch your mind off from football."

BALE'S SUPER SKILLS

One of the best players on the planet to watch, the Welshman doesn't have any weaknesses in his game.

Bale's brilliant left foot make him one of the feared free-kick takers in the business.

FREE KICK GENIUS

The sight of Bale lining up a free-kick is a nightmare for goalkeepers because of the variety the Welsh star can produce from a dead ball. Even he admits he doesn't always know what the ball is going to do in the air once he has hit it. The number of times goalkeepers are left completely wrong-footed by his shots proves just how difficult it is to guess how the ball is going to travel.

TOUGH TACKLER

The Welshman started out as a full-back so it's no surprise that even though he's known as a flair player, he's also one of the best tacklers around. His natural pace often gets him in the right position to win the ball, but it is his superb technique in contact that makes the big difference.

A superb athlete Bale can outjump and beat much taller defenders.

HEAD BOY

Bale stands 1.83m (6ft) tall and although most defenders are taller, Bale regularly scores for club and country with headers. His ability to leap above bigger men, hang in the air and then power the ball home with his head is amazing and gives him another important attacking weapon.

AMAZING ACCELERATION

Bale's speed is legendary, but it's his pace over the first five metres that is really deadly, leaving defenders completely stranded. "It's massively important to my game," he says. "If you've got that explosive acceleration, you're able to get away from defenders and either shoot and score, pass or cross. It gives you an extra advantage."

DAZZLING DRIBBLING

Pace means nothing if you can't control the ball and it is Bale's unbelievable ability to keep at it his feet even when he is at top speed that has made him a global superstar. "To dribble past defenders you need to believe in your ability and trust your instincts," he says. "From a technical point of view, keep your eye on the ball, but take quick snapshots of what's in front of you so that you can react. Keep the ball close and take nice firm, controlled touches – not too soft, not too heavy."

Few players can live with the Welshman's frightening pace when he's in full flow.

GREAT MADRID GOALS

Here are six of the best from Gareth Bale since he signed for Real.

REAL MADRID 7 v SEVILLA 3
La Liga, 30 October 2013

Bale celebrated his first La Liga start at the Bernabeu in style as Madrid ran riot. He scored twice, the first of which was a cracker, collecting Karim Benzema's clever pass just inside the box before powering a beautiful, curling left-footed shot into the top corner.

REAL MADRID 3 v ELCHE 0
La Liga, 22 February 2014

Bale's incredible goal against Elche had to be seen to be believed. Madrid were all over Elche, who struggled to clear the danger and the ball fell to Bale, fully 45 yards out. He looked up and unleashed a devastating shot that rocketed past the stunned goalkeeper Manu Herrera, off the crossbar and into the net.

Bale's goal in 2014 saw Madrid win their 19th Copa del Rey.

BARCELONA 1 v REAL MADRID 2
Copa del Rey final, 16 April 2014

A stunning solo goal in the 85th minute which won the final for Real, Bale was still inside his own half when he picked up the ball and pushed it past a Barca defender. The Welshman hit the gas, but his path was blocked, so he sprinted off the pitch and around the obstacle before coolly beating the keeper from close range.

REAL MADRID 4 v ATLETICO MADRID 1
UEFA Champions League final, 24 May 2014

There is no bigger stage in club football than the UEFA Champions League final and Bale delivered when it really mattered. With the score at 1–1, ten minutes from the end of extra-time, he appeared at the back post to slam home an unstoppable header from Angel di Maria's deflected cross.

In 2014, Bale became the first Welshman to score in a European Cup or UEFA Champions League final.

REAL MADRID 3 v ESPANYOL 0
La Liga, 10 January 2015

Cristiano Ronaldo stepped aside to let Bale take this free kick at the Bernabeu and the Welshman made the most of his chance, producing a gorgeous effort which flew over the wall, smacked against the post and rippled the net.

REAL MADRID 5 v DEPORTIVO DE LA CORUNA 0
La Liga, 9 January 2016

This was Zinedine Zidane's first game as Madrid manager and Bale showed his new boss all his outrageous skills with a brilliant hat-trick. The pick of the bunch was his second – his 50th goal for the club – side-footing Cristiano Ronaldo's right wing cross into the net from the edge of the area.

Bale reached his half century of goals for Los Blancos in 2016.

TRAINING WITH BALE

Fast, super fit and incredibly strong, the Welshman is constantly working hard behind the scenes to ensure he stays at the top of his game.

Natural talent is a vital ingredient to becoming a world-class star but it's the hours spent on the training ground that separate the great from the good and few players are as dedicated as Bale when it comes to getting into shape.

In his early days at Spurs, he suffered knee and ankle injuries which put him on the sidelines, but he soon realised that a full summer of training could solve the problem and make him much stronger.

"If you don't complete preseason, you're 80 percent more likely to get injured during the season," he said. "It's also an opportunity for the manager to work on tactics and formations and get his ideas and across so that everybody knows what is expected of them and what their jobs are."

Today the Bernabeu hero is one of the fittest and most powerful players in La Liga and his training regime is specially designed to get him match ready.

"The best way to train is by replicating what you do in a game; repeated sprints across the length of the pitch," he said.

Bale has thrived in Spain under the leadership of Bernabeu boss Zinedine Zidane (in background).

OCTOBER 2012
Scored twice in an international for the first time, his brace earning Wales a 2–1 victory over Scotland in a 2014 World Cup qualifier.

FEBRUARY 2013
Registered the 10th goal of his Wales career in a 1–0 friendly win over Austria in Swansea, becoming the 17th Welshman to reach double figures in international football.

JUNE 2016
On target in Wales' Group B opener against Slovakia in Bordeaux at Euro 2016, he became the first Welshman to score in the European Championship finals and the first in a major tournament for 58 years.

NOVEMBER 2016
Scored in a 1–1 draw with Serbia in a 2018 World Cup qualifier. The goal took his tally for 2016 to seven, making it his most prolific international year.

BALE IN NUMBERS

All the stats you need to know about the flying Welsh wizard.

55 The number of goals Bale scored for Spurs in all competitions in his six seasons with the London club. His best year was his last, netting 26 times in 44 appearances in 2012–13.

11.4 Seconds it took the speedster to run the 100 metres when he was a teenager at school in Cardiff.

38 Minutes it took the Welshman to open his Real Madrid account. He scored on his debut for Los Blancos against Villarreal in September 2013.

10 Goals scored by Bale in Euro 2016 qualifying matches (seven) and the finals (three).

20,000 Supporters in the Bernabeu to watch Bale's official unveiling as a Madrid player in 2013.

13 Number of games it took Bale to register his first hat-trick for Real Madrid – his treble coming against Valladolid in November 2013.

16 His age in years (plus 275 days) when he made his senior debut for Southampton, against Millwall in April 2006.

7 Major trophies that Gareth Bale has helped Real Madrid to win in his first four seasons in Spain.

3 Times he won the Premier League Player of the Month award (in April 2010, January 2012 and February 2013) and times he was also named in the PFA Premier League Team of the Year (2010–11, 2011–12 and 2012–13).

BALE'S SUPERSTAR TEAM-MATES

The Welsh wizard isn't the only world-class player on show at the Bernabeu. Here are four of Bale's fellow Madrid greats.

KARIM BENZEMA

Bale and Ronaldo make up a dazzling attacking duo, but Benzema gives Madrid a terrifying trio and ever since the French striker arrived at the Bernabeu in 2009, he has been banging in the goals regularly. Big and powerful, he is a real handful for defences. Benzema's Real scoring record is amazing: more than 100 in La Liga; more than 40 in European football, and his goal-tally has reached double figures in all eight seasons in Spain.

SERGIO RAMOS

Signed in 2005, the Spain defender is the longest-serving current player at the Bernabeu, with more than 500 appearances. Ramos has been Real's club captain since 2015 and has won three La Liga titles, and two each of the FIFA Club World Cup, UEFA Champions League, UEFA Super Cup and Copa del Rey since joining Real. His greatest moment was when he captained the club to glory in the 2016 Champions League final in Milan against city rivals Atletico Madrid.

TONI KROOS

The midfielder was a World Cup winner with Germany in 2014 and joined Madrid soon after. A playmaker with the ability to unlock even the tightest defence with his brilliant range of passing, Kroos has won the UEFA Champions League and two FIFA Club World Cups since moving to Spain and his superb performances in the heart of the Real midfield saw also him named in the 2016 UEFA Team of the Year.

CRISTIANO RONALDO

The similarities between Bale and Ronaldo are striking: both players boast incredible skill, pace and power, and if it isn't the Welshman terrorising defences, his Portuguese team-mate is always on hand to do the damage. Ronaldo is Real's all-time top scorer with more than 380 goals and also the UEFA Champions League's deadliest striker. Since signing for Los Blancos from Manchester United in 2009, Ronaldo has helped the club lift nine major trophies.

BALE'S ARMY OF FANS

One of the most famous sportsmen on the planet, the Welshman is adored by millions of football supporters around the world.

The game's great entertainers are always the most popular with the public and Bale's explosive performances for club and country have ensured his every move on and off the pitch is closely followed by his huge number of fans.

He is already a legend in Spain after his move to Madrid in 2013 and he has long been a national hero at home in Wales, where he is now regarded as the greatest player the country has ever produced.

Bale's world record £85 million transfer to Real was a turning point in terms of his fame, making headlines all over the world, but it was during Euro 2016 that he became a true superstar as Wales reached the semi-finals.

By the end of the group stages, of all the players participating at the tournament, Bale's name was the most searched-for online, and when the tournament was over, his official Facebook page was also in the top three ranked by the "most likes", "shares" and "comments".

His popularity on all forms of social media is amazing. His Facebook page had received more than 28.5 million likes by the end of

Bale has become a firm favourite with the Real Madrid faithful since his world record move to the Bernabeu.

February 2017, while his Instagram account had more than 27 million followers. Another 11 million followed him on Twitter, while even an unofficial "Gareth Bale Fans Club" has two million-plus likes.

In November 2016, a new social media network was launched, called "Dugout", and one of the first players they signed up was Bale, promising to bring his army of fans exclusive behind-the-scenes footage and videos.

It is though in Wales that his most passionate fans can be found. This love for their favourite son was underlined during Euro 2016, when the town of Bala, in North Wales, renamed itself "Bale" in a tribute to him.

The Welsh town of Bala changed its named during Euro 2016 to honour their hero.

Bale, one of the world's most famous footballers, spends hours signing autographs for his fans.

PLAYING FOR REAL MADRID

After a sensational 2012–13 season for Spurs, Gareth Bale headed to Spain in a mega deal which smashed the world transfer record.

Real Madrid have always attracted football's biggest and brightest stars and, in the summer of 2013, the club made the Welshman the game's then most expensive player when they signed him from Tottenham for approximately £86 million. The Spanish giants had paid around £80 million for Cristiano Ronaldo four years earlier, but broke their own club record with the fee to bring Bale to the Bernabeu.

"I have had six very happy years at Tottenham but it's the right time to say goodbye," Bale said. "I am now looking forward to the next exciting chapter in my life, playing football for Real Madrid. I know many players talk of their desire to join the club of their boyhood dreams, but I can honestly say, this is my dream come true."

Gareth Bale holds up his new Real Madrid shirt with Real President Florentino Perez in 2013.

Bale poses with the UEFA Champions League trophy at the Estadio da Luz in Lisbon in May 2014.

The 24-year-old signed a six-year deal, and was handed the number 11 shirt. It didn't take him long to make his mark, scoring on his debut against Villarreal in La Liga. It was just the start of what was a brilliant first season.

In October he scored twice and set up two more as Real demolished Sevilla 7–3 at the Bernabeu. His man of the match display earned him the nickname "The Cannon" in the Spanish newspapers. Bale's first Madrid hat-trick came the following month against Real Valladolid.

The goals continued to flow for the Welshman and he became a true hero with the Madrid fans when he was on target five minutes before the final whistle in the final of the Copa del Rey in April, scoring the winner against arch-rivals Barcelona. It was an amazing individual goal, Bale sprinting past the defence from the half-way line before beating the keeper.

Bale outpaces Fernando Navarro of Seville during the UEFA Super Cup match at Cardiff City Stadium in 2014.

The 2–1 victory gave Bale the first winner's medal of his career and, in May, he doubled his collection as Real claimed the UEFA Champions League trophy for a record 10th time. Los Blancos played local rivals Atletico Madrid in Lisbon in the final and the winger was in brilliant form, scoring Real's second goal, ten minutes from the end of extra time, with a powerful header at the back post. His strike took his tally for his new club in his debut season to 22 goals in all competitions, plus 16 assists. Real went on to win 4–1.

"This will live with me forever," Bale said after the final. "It is what every footballer dreams of and it doesn't come bigger in club football. The celebration of the crowd meant everything to me. The most important thing is we worked hard as a team and won the trophy."

The 2014–15 season saw Madrid kick-off with a UEFA Super Cup clash against Sevilla in Cardiff and Bale showed, back in his hometown, that he was as deadly as ever, setting up Ronaldo for the first goal of the match. Real ran out 2–0 winners and, barely a year after leaving England, he had helped the club lift three major trophies.

He continued to bang in the goals in La Liga, including a brace against Deportivo La Coruna in September, but he was even better when Real

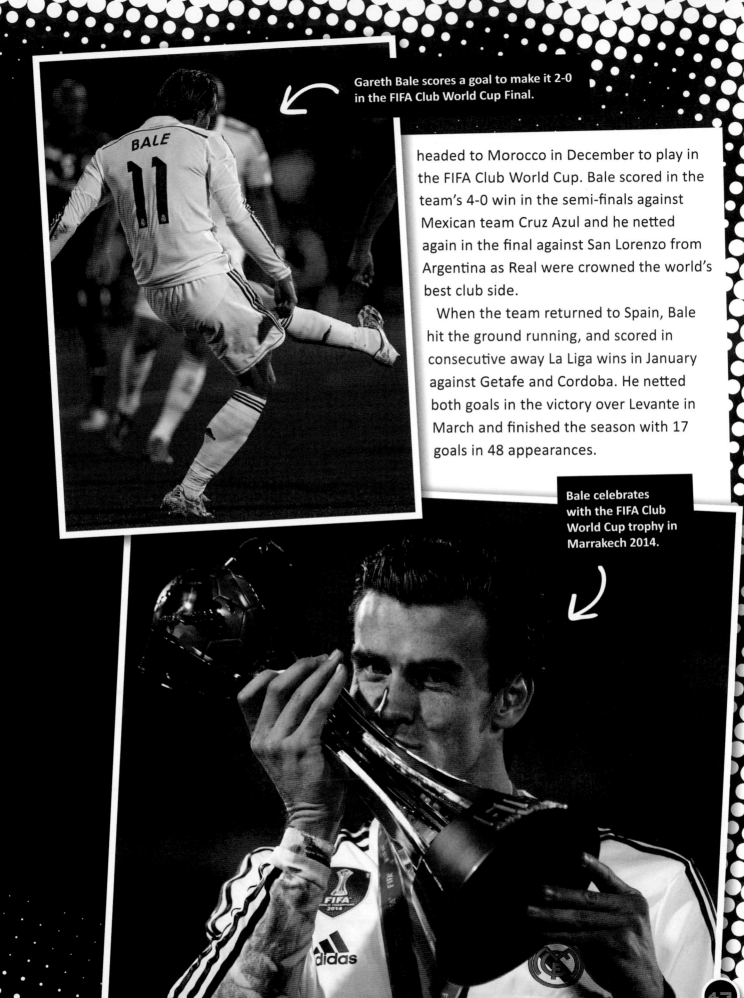

Gareth Bale scores a goal to make it 2-0 in the FIFA Club World Cup Final.

headed to Morocco in December to play in the FIFA Club World Cup. Bale scored in the team's 4-0 win in the semi-finals against Mexican team Cruz Azul and he netted again in the final against San Lorenzo from Argentina as Real were crowned the world's best club side.

When the team returned to Spain, Bale hit the ground running, and scored in consecutive away La Liga wins in January against Getafe and Cordoba. He netted both goals in the victory over Levante in March and finished the season with 17 goals in 48 appearances.

Bale celebrates with the FIFA Club World Cup trophy in Marrakech 2014.

Bale tussles with Barcelona's Javier Mascherano during their November 2015 La Liga match at the Bernabeu.

Bale poses after signing his contract extension with the club until 2022 at Estadio Santiago Bernabeu in 2016.

His third season in Spain started with a bang as Bale helped himself to a brace in a 5–0 win against Real Betis in September 2015. It was the 200th goal scored by Madrid's unstoppable attacking trio of Bale, Ronaldo and Karim Benzema since the three had first played together two years earlier.

In December, he scored four goals in a match for the first time in his professional career as Madrid smashed Rayo Vallecano 10–2 in La Liga. But it was in the UEFA Champions League final in Milan in May that Bale shone when it really mattered.

For the second time in two years, Atletico Madrid were Real's opponents and it was Bale who was the creator of the first goal of the final, flicking on Toni Kroos' free-kick with a header which captain Sergio Ramos converted from close range.

The match finished 1–1 after extra-time and went to a penalty shootout. Bale held his nerve with Madrid's third spot-kick, cleverly sending the goalkeeper the wrong way. Los Blancos won the shoot-out 5–3 to become the Europe's champion club for a record-extending 11th time.

It was business as usual for Bale in 2016–17, starting the new season with a brilliant double against Real Sociedad in the club's La Liga opener. He was on target again in October against Eibar, his strike in front of a sold out Bernabeu giving him his 50th league goal for the Los Blancos.

There was more reason to celebrate at the end of the month when Madrid announced Bale had signed a new deal which would keep him in Spain until 2022, meaning the Real faithful will enjoy many more seasons watching the Welsh wizard in action.

In November Bale suffered an ankle injury that kept him out of action until February and a calf injury in April was another blow. Nonetheless, he did celebrate another La Liga title, Madrid's 33rd, and he was back in time for Real's UEFA Champions League final in his hometown of Cardiff in June.

Bale was a substitute for the Juventus clash, but he came on in the 77th minute as Madrid stormed to a 4–1 victory in the Principality Stadium. He thus lifted the famous trophy for the third time in his career – this time in the city where it all started.

REAL HERO

The first Welshman ever to play for Los Blancos, it didn't take Gareth Bale long to win over the Bernabeu faithful after his big-money-move to Spain.

Real Madrid fans demand two things – style and success – and ever since his world-record transfer from Spurs in the summer of 2013, Bale has given them both. He arrived at the Bernabeu with a reputation as big as his price tag, and he has not disappointed.

No club has won La Liga more times than Real's 33 successes, but Bale's first season at the Bernabeu was all about the team's pursuit of a record-breaking 10th Champions League trophy, known as La Decima.

It had been 12 long years since Madrid had last been crowned champions of Europe, but Bale proved to be the final piece of the jigsaw as Carlo Ancelotti's side finally ended the wait for the biggest prize in club football.

Bale's European performances that season were brilliant, scoring six times in 12 appearances, as well as providing four assists, and with each game Real supporters fell further in love with their new signing.

He saved his best for last and the final against Atletico Madrid in Lisbon. The derby match was a tight one and went into extra time and with just 10 minutes left, the game was heading to a penalty shootout, only for Bale to score with a back-post header to break Atletico's stubborn resistance. In only his first season with Madrid Bale had become a club legend.

Bale's all-action style has made him one of La Liga's most dangerous attacking players.

The goals have flowed regularly for the record-breaking Welshman in Spain.

Two years later the Welshman was again in fabulous form as Los Blancos won their 11th Champions League. Bale was on the scoresheet again, converting Real's third penalty in a shootout in the final against Atletico to earn his second's winner's medal.

And two became three in 2017 when Real outclassed Juventus 4–1 in the Champions League final in Cardiff, their 12th win being five more than any other club. Bale recovered from injury to play 13 minutes in his hometown to join an exclusive club of players with three Champions League winners' medals.

Although he saw limited action in the 2017 Champions League final, Bale did help Real Madrid defeat Juventus 4–1 in Cardiff.

Bale's stunning free-kick gave Wales a half-time lead against England at Lens, but England hit back to win 2-1.

EUROPEAN HERO

Wales' magnificent march to the semi-finals of Euro 2016 was the story of the tournament and Bale was on fire in the finals in France.

Welsh football fans had waited a very, very, long time to see their team in action in a major tournament finals. The country hadn't qualified for an international competition finals since the 1958 World Cup (although Wales were in the last eight of the 1976 European Championship, the finals started with the last four) but with Bale at his brilliant best, the summer of 2016 finally saw Wales back on the big stage.

Bale was in amazing form in qualifying, scoring seven goals. But it was when the finals kicked off that he really exploded into life as Chris Coleman's underdogs went almost all the way to the final.

Wales were drawn in Group B with England, Slovakia and Russia, and Bale started the tournament in style with a deadly, long-range free-kick against Slovakia in Marseille after 10 minutes which set up a 2–1 win.

Five days later, Wales faced England in Lens and although they lost the match, Bale was on target again with another unbelievable free-kick, this one from 40 yards out, which flew into the bottom left-hand corner of Joe Hart's goal.

Wales needed to beat Russia in Toulouse to reach the knock-out stages and Bale made it three goals in three games with a cool, second-half finish to seal a comfortable 3–0 victory.

In the last 16, Wales met Northern Ireland and although Bale didn't score, it was his dangerous, left-footed cross which defender Gareth McAuley turned into his own net.

Against all the odds, Wales were through to the quarter-finals and no-one expected them to beat Belgium. Bale and his team-mates, however, had other ideas and, after 90 minutes of drama, Wales were 3-1 winners. It was the most famous victory in the history of Welsh football.

Their Euro 2016 fairytale finally came to an end in the semi-final in Lyon as Portugal won 2–0 but

Bale's three goals in France earned him a place in the record books as Wales' all-time top scorer in a major tournament finals.

Gareth Bale and his Wales team-mates line up before the UEFA Euro 2016 quarter-final victory over Belgium.

Bale celebrates the 3-1 quarter-final defeat of much-fancied Belgium.

BALE AND HIS COACHES

The flying Welsh winger has played for some of the game's greatest managers on his journey to becoming a global superstar.

GEORGE BURLEY

The man who gave Bale his professional debut as a teenager at Southampton, the Scot's calming influence was crucial in the early days of his career. Burley made sure there was no pressure on the youngster and Bale responded by helping the Saints into the 2006–07 Championship play-offs.

"HE WAS ALWAYS A SPECIAL PLAYER. HE ALWAYS HAD ALL THE ATTRIBUTES TO BECOME A WORLD-CLASS PLAYER."

"HE IS THE KIND OF FOOTBALLER WHO CAN RISE TO THE OCCASION IN BIG GAMES."

HARRY
"I think he together Redknapp convinced that in to fully be the best in the 2009–10 season qualified for

CARLO ANCELOTTI

The Italian's years of managerial experience were vital when Bale headed to Spain in 2013 and had to come to terms with his world record transfer fee. The new signing rewarded his manager's faith with a brilliant debut season in which Madrid won the Champions League.

"I THINK HE STANDS NOW WITH LIONEL MESSI, CRISTIANO RONALDO AND LUIS SUAREZ AS ONE OF THE BEST FOUR PLAYERS IN THE WORLD."

CHRIS COLEMAN

The duo are a match made in heaven and since Coleman became coach of Wales in 2012, it has been a golden era for the team. Bale loves playing for his fellow Welshman, scoring seven goals in qualifying to send the side into the Euro 2016 finals.

"HE IS A TOP, TOP PLAYER AND WE ARE SO, SO FORTUNATE TO HAVE HIM. OTHER PLAYERS COULD LOOK AT GARETH AND LEARN SO MUCH."

"HE MAKES THINGS LOOK EASY. HIS PACE IS FRIGHTENING. HIS ACCELERATION IS UNBELIEVABLE BECAUSE OF HIS ABILITY TO GO THROUGH THE GEARS IN VERY LITTLE SPACE."

ZINEDINE ZIDANE

Bale scored a hat-trick in Zidane's first game as Madrid manager in January 2016 and ever since the Frenchman got the job, Bale has been in unstoppable form. Together the pair have already won the UEFA Champions League twice, the FIFA Club World Cup and the UEFA Super Cup.

51

GREAT WALES GOALS

Here are six of Gareth Bale's best goals playing for his country.

Bale's second goal against Scotland in October 2012 was his ninth for Wales in 37 international appearances.

WALES 2 v SCOTLAND 1
World Cup Qualifier, 12 October 2012

Scotland goalkeeper Allan McGregor looked worried as Bale powered towards goal in the 88th minute in Cardiff. He was right to be nervous as Bale unleashed a long range, left-footed drive that screamed across him and into the top corner to win the match.

WALES 2 v AUSTRIA 1
Friendly, 6 February 2013

Midfielder Joe Allen supplied a brilliant long pass from his own half and Bale brought the ball down with a sensational first touch. He then sped towards goal and scored with a low left-foot drive from the edge of the box which flew the bottom corner.

WALES 3 u ICELAND 1
Friendly, 5 March 2014
Bale was in his own half when he got possession, but Iceland simply couldn't stop him as he sprinted past one helpless defender outside the touchline, raced towards goal and threaded a low shot between three more defenders into the back of the net.

There was a double celebration for Bale against Belgium in Cardiff in 2015; his 50th Welsh cap and the winning goal.

WALES 1 u BELGIUM 0
Euro 2016 Qualifier, 12 June 2015
This goal sent Wales to the top of their qualifying group. Belgium failed to properly clear the ball from their area and Bale was in exactly the right place at the right time to superbly chest down the ball, swivel and shoot, right-footed, past Thibaut Courtois.

This "Bale Special' free-kick against Slovakia started his and Wales's dream run to the UEFA Euro 2016 semi-finals.

GLOBAL SUPERSTAR

One of the most famous and photographed players on the planet, Gareth Bale is recognised wherever he travels in the world.

Real Madrid is the biggest club in the game and Bale one of the poster boys of the team. His amazing talent, attacking style and good looks have ensured he is incredibly popular with football fans all over the world.

In 2016, he was named the highest ranked British athlete in the "ESPN World Fame 100" list, ahead of tennis star Andy Murray, top golfer Rory McIlroy and three-time Formula One world champion Lewis Hamilton, while he has millions of followers from hundreds of different countries on social media.

His amazing form – and three goals – for Wales at Euro 2016 in France only increased his profile and the following year Bale hit the big screen when a documentary film Don't Take Me Home – all about the team's incredible journey to the semi-finals – was released in cinemas.

Bale's brilliance on the pitch has earned him millions of pounds off it in sponsorship and advertising deals and, in 2015, he was ranked as one of the top 10 most marketable footballers in Europe.

His deals include endorsements for companies like Adidas, Lucozade and BT Sport and in 2014 he appeared alongside Barcelona player Lionel Messi on the cover of the game FIFA 14. He has also worked for car giant Nissan, Sony Mobile and Foot Locker Europe.

The Welshman was famous even before he signed for Madrid and it was a picture of him – in a Tottenham shirt – on a giant billboard that hung in Times Square in New York City in 2013 when TV station NBC advertised their coverage of the Premier League.

Another sign of Bale's popularity is the number of replica Madrid shirts featuring his name and number that have been sold since he arrived in Spain. Thousands of fans bought number 11 shirts when he signed in 2013 and, in 2016, he broke into the top 10 of best-selling players by leading sport retailer Kitbag.

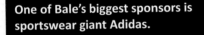
One of Bale's biggest sponsors is sportswear giant Adidas.

Bale (middle) and his Wales team-mates celebrated with an open top bus ride after Euro 2016.

Bale was on a Times Square billboard to promote NBC's Premier League coverage.

RECORD BREAKER

Although his best years are still ahead of him, Bale has already rewritten the record books during his brilliant club and international career.

When Bale scored Real Madrid's second goal in their 4–1 victory over Atletico Madrid in the 2014 UEFA Champions League final, he became the first Welsh player ever to score in European club football's biggest game. Ian Rush had been on target in the 1984 final for Liverpool against Roma but that was in a penalty shootout.

Winning the UEFA Champions League for a third time in 2017 made Bale the most successful Welshman in the competition, going ahead of Joey Jones and Ryan Giggs who both won it twice.

When the Welshman scored for Real in their 4–0 win against Sevilla in March 2016 it took his tally in La Liga to 43 goals, passing England striker Gary Lineker's – 42 goals in 103 Barcelona appearances, 1986–89 – previous British record in Spain.

Bale's three goals in France in UEFA Euro 2016 made him Wales' top scorer of all time in the finals of a major tournament. His strikes against Slovakia, England and Russia took him past Ivor Allchurch who netted two goals in the 1958

The £85.3million move from Tottenham to Real Madrid in the summer of 2013 made Bale the most expensive player in football history at the time. The deal broke Real's own record, set in 2009, when they paid Manchester United £80million to bring Cristiano Ronaldo from Old Trafford to the Bernabeu. Bale's record was overtaken in the 2016 when United spent £89.3million to sign French midfielder Paul Pogba from Juventus.

INSIDE THE TROPHY CABINET

Bale has picked up seven winner's medals since signing for Real Madrid. Here's how the great midfielder became a multiple champion.

REAL MADRID 2 v BARCELONA 1
Copa del Rey final, 16 April 2014

Los Blancos lifted the Copa del Rey for the 19th time thanks to Bale's stunning winner late in the second half. Angel di Maria had given Madrid an early lead, only for defender Marc Bartra to equalise for Barca, setting the stage for Bale's incredible break from inside his own half five minutes from time.

ATLETICO MADRID 1 v REAL MADRID 4
UEFA Champions League final, 29 May 2014

The all-Spanish – and all-Madrid – final was held in the Portuguese capital of Lisbon and it was a classic. Madrid seemed to be heading for defeat until Sergio Ramos equalised in second-half injury time. In extra time, Los Blancos ran riot as Bale gave Real a 110th-minute lead and Marcelo and Cristiano Ronaldo added further goals.

The 2014 Copa del Rey was the first silverware of Bale's senior career, and his great goal beat Barcelona.

REAL MADRID 2 v SEVILLA 0
UEFA Super Cup, 12 August 2014

The Welshman headed to his hometown of Cardiff for the UEFA Super Cup and it was his stunning left-footed cross that set up Cristiano Ronaldo for his second goal as Los Blancos lifted the trophy for a third time.

SAN LORENZO 0 v REAL MADRID 2
FIFA Club World Cup final, 20 December 2014

Bale had already scored in the FIFA Club World Cup semi-final against Mexico's Cruz Azul and he was on target again in the final as Real were crowned the world's best club side. Six minutes into the second half in Morocco's Stade de Marrakech, Bale's left-foot strike from the edge of the area added to Sergio Ramos' 37th-minute opener to give Real a 2–0 win.

REAL MADRID 1 v ATLETICO MADRID 1
Champions League, 28 May 2016

More than 70,000 fans packed into the San Siro in Milan for the 2016 Champions League final and a showdown between the cross-city rivals. Sergio Ramos gave Real a 15th-minute lead, but Yannick Carrasco equalised for Atletico 11 minutes from time. In the penalty shoot-out Bale scored with Real's third attempt as they won 5–3.

MALAGA 0 v REAL MADRID 2
La Liga, 21 May 2017

Injury forced Bale to watch his team-mates wrap up a 33rd league title for Los Blancos from the sidelines but with 19 appearances and seven goals in the 2016–17 La Liga season, he had played a massive part in the side's success.

JUVENTUS 1 v REAL MADRID 4
Champions League final, 3 June 2017

Madrid were magical in Cardiff as they overpowered the Italian champions to become champions of Europe for the 12th time. Bale came off the bench in the second half to join the celebrations.

Bale is all smiles after Real Madrid had won the UEFA Champions League for the 12th time in 2017.

WHAT NEXT FOR BALE?

With a bumper new contract, a young family and his best years of football ahead of him, the future is bright for Gareth Bale.

Great players are always in demand and after helping Madrid win a La Liga and Champions League double in 2016–17, Bale was again one of the most wanted men in European football.

Manchester United were believed to be ready to break the bank with a big-money transfer to bring him back to the Premier League but Real had already made their move and offered their star player a new, six-year contract.

It didn't take Bale long to make up his mind and in November 2016 the Welshman signed the deal which will keep him at the Bernabeu until 2022 when he will be 33-years-old. It now looks like Bale will spend the rest of his record-breaking career at the Bernabeu.

"Real Madrid is the best club in the world and when you have the opportunity to play here you cannot waste it," he said. "I extended my contract because I feel very happy. Every year I am more confident, and I think we can keep winning titles. All titles are important and we want to win every competition we play in.

"My life has changed a lot in this time because it has made me grow as a person. These have been three wonderful years and I hope there are six more wonderful years. I will always fight for this club. I have enjoyed every experience, the fans love me and I will try to win all the titles that I can."

With his future sorted, Bale can now focus on his football and setting even more records for club and country. Another Champions League victory with Los Blancos would see him become only the second British player ever to lift the trophy four

Bale will be a star attraction at Real Madrid for many more seasons after he signed his new deal in November 2016.

Bale's arrival in Madrid has seen the club win the Champions League three times, including in both 2016 and 2017.

Bale is targeting even more silverware in the next six seasons at the Bernabeu.

times while, with 17 more goals, he would also become the highest scoring Welshman in the history of the tournament, passing Ryan Giggs' mark of 30 goals.

At age 27, if he plays international football for five more years, to World Cup 2022, he will surely shatter the Welsh record for both appearances (92, by Neville Southall) and goals (Ian Rush, 28).

QUIZ TIME

Here are 20 questions to test your knowledge of the Real Madrid and Wales star.

1 In which city was Gareth Bale born on 16 July 1989?

2 How old was he when making his professional debut for Southampton against Millwall?

3. Who was the Saints' manager in the 2006–07 season?

4. Against which club did Bale make his Premier League debut for Spurs?

5. In which competition did the Welshman score his first career hat-trick in 2010?

6. How many times did Bale win England's PFA Player of the Year Award?

7. How many goals did Bale score in his six seasons at Spurs?

8. In what year did Real Madrid break the world record transfer fee by signing Bale?

9. Who was his first manager at the Bernabeu?

10. Against which club did Bale score his first goal for *Los Blancos*?

11. In which competition did Bale win his first trophy with Madrid in April 2014??

12. What was the final score when Bale's Madrid beat Atletico Madrid in the 2014 Champions League final?

13. In which city did Bale win the 2016 Champions League final with *Los Blancos*?

14. When will Bale's latest contract with Real, signed in 2016, run out?

15. Bale made his international debut for Wales in 2006 in a friendly against which country?

16. How many times has Bale won the Wales Footballer of the Year Award?

17. Bale's Euro 2016 finals goals came against Slovakia, England and which other country?

18. Bale broke which British player's record for most goals in La Liga in 2016?

19. Alongside which La Liga player did Bale appear on the cover of the FIFA 14 game?

20. How many trophies had Bale won with Madrid by the end of the 2016–17 season?